Through Otis' Eyes

Through Otis' Eyes

Eyes

*Lessons from a
Guide Dog Puppy*

BY PATRICIA BURLIN KENNEDY

ILLUSTRATED BY ROBERT CHRISTIE

HOWELL BOOK HOUSE

MACMILLAN • USA

Howell Book House
A Simon & Schuster Macmillan Company
1633 Broadway
New York, NY 10019

Macmillan Publishing books may be purchased for business or sales promotional use. For information please write: Special Markets Department, Macmillan Publishing USA, 1633 Broadway, New York, NY 10019.

Library of Congress Cataloging-in-Publication Data
Kennedy, Patricia Burlin.
Through Otis' eyes: lessons from a guide dog puppy / by Patricia Burlin Kennedy;
illustrated by Robert Christie.
p. cm.
ISBN: 0-87605-473-4
1. Guide dogs.   2. Puppies.   I. Title.
HV1780.K45   1997
362.4'183—dc21   97-25723
CIP

Manufactured in the United States of America

10 9 8 7 6 5 4 3 2 1

BOOK AND COVER DESIGN BY KEVIN HANEK

This book is dedicated to the remarkable

animals who inspired it.

— P.B.K.

For my grandchildren Michael, Lauren and Cole.

— R.C.

Acknowledgments

I AM VERY GRATEFUL to my husband Kevin and to my family and friends who have encouraged and supported me in this project. Special thanks to Deedee Schur for her unflagging enthusiasm. I would also like to express my gratitude to the staff and volunteers of Guiding Eyes for the Blind, Inc., particularly Louise Schofield, Judy McKinley, Cheryl O'Connor, Linda Deam, Suzi Gatipon and Deb Clark. Thank you also to Dr. Richard Weitzman for generously donating his veterinary services during Otis' first year.

I feel very fortunate that Bob Christie was willing to devote his time and talent to bring Otis to life in the pages of *Through Otis' Eyes*. I hope that through his beautiful and expressive illustrations, readers can experience or relive the joys and frustrations of bringing up a young Labrador Retriever.

Finally, I would like to thank my editor, Jennifer Liberts, for sharing my vision for "Otis."

A portion of the proceeds will be donated to Guiding Eyes for the Blind, Inc.

Introduction

Otis entered my life in May of 1994. An adorable, rambunctious seven-week-old Black Labrador Retriever puppy, he arrived at our door in the arms of a staff member of Guiding Eyes for the Blind, Inc. (GEB). Born to "Timber" and "Sailor" on St. Patrick's Day at the GEB Breeding Center in New York, Otis and his "O" littermates (Orchid, Osborne, Oboe, Otto, Owen, O'Neill and Olive) were puppies with a very special purpose. They were bred to become the partners of blind persons seeking fuller, more independent lives. But first, they had to grow up. When our family volunteered to raise a puppy, we were matched with Otis, who was to spend his first year with us. This book is a reflection on that year and the lessons Otis taught me as I watched him grow and prepare for a life of service.

Early on, guide dog puppies are evaluated on how well they "tune in" to their handlers. As Otis grew, I noticed some reversal in our roles. I was also "tuning in" to Otis. It dawned on me that Otis' innate talent for living could be, when personified, ideals to strive for in my life—to love unconditionally, to forgive without question, to live in the present moment, to give of one's time without hesitation or regret. Although Otis began his life as a prospective guide dog, his lessons are not unique to working animals. They should be familiar to anyone who has ever let a dog into their home or their heart.

My husband Kevin, son Tommy, daughter Katie and Golden Retriever Bailey shared in the experience of raising Otis. When we were considering fostering a puppy, the question we asked was, "How can we give him up?" Having lost a beloved Golden Retriever to cancer months before, we wondered if we were setting ourselves up for another heartbreak. Representatives of the school told us that the kind of persons they were seeking to raise their puppies would, by virtue of their affection for the animals, find it difficult to say good-bye after a year. Parting would be easier, they added, if we kept in mind from the beginning that our puppy was "different." Consequently, when given the choice between a Golden Retriever, Yellow or Black Labrador Retriever or German Shepherd, we asked for a Black Lab, thus ensuring that our puppy even looked different from our surviving Golden.

Once Otis arrived, we became part of a community of about fifty local puppy raisers, supported by GEB staff and volunteer area coordinators, bound together by our love for the dogs and the bittersweet nature of our common purpose. Through socialization classes, receptions with blind "graduates" and their guide dogs, visits to the training center and fundraising events, we were constantly reminded of the important role our puppies would play in the lives of others.

I was often moved by the extraordinary people I met through the program. There were raisers who had physical impairments of their own, but who gave of themselves so that others might have more fulfilling lives. There was a blind woman with a guide dog who visited nursing homes to lead residents in musical movement sessions. These acts of selflessness touched me deeply. I was also constantly inspired by the remarkable stories and accomplishments of the blind persons I met during Otis' first year.

And, there were wonderful moments. I will never forget the reunion of an elderly guide dog, whose blind partner had recently died, with the family who had raised her. After many years of devoted service, she was to live out her life in the place where it began. I am still moved by a conversation I had with a blind man who worked for an emergency relief agency. He emotionally spoke of the search and rescue dogs helping the victims of the

Oklahoma City bombing. And, I will always remember the warm smiles that greeted Otis once he earned his "puppy jacket" and we were able to visit public places to expose him to new situations. He truly brought out the best in people.

The day we had been dreading arrived in June of 1995. We tearfully said good-bye to Otis and sent him back to be reunited with his siblings at the GEB Training School. This is where the hard work begins. Since this book was written from a puppy raiser's perspective, it does not attempt to portray the months of intensive training required to transform a young energetic dog into a reliable guide. Nor can *Through Otis' Eyes* adequately reflect the bond that develops between the dedicated trainers and the dogs they teach to be the eyes of a blind person. Certainly, I cannot begin to convey the experience of a blind student meeting his guide dog for the first time, nor the month they spend together working to become a team.

Words and illustrations can only hint at the heartfelt emotions present at graduation ceremonies celebrating the accomplishments of the new teams. In addition to the family members and friends of the graduates, puppy raisers are invited to see the dogs they returned to school in harness with their new companions. The blind graduates and the raisers then share stories and memories about the dogs who brought them together. A more powerful and rewarding experience is hard to imagine.

Through Otis' eyes I see

the wonder

and excitement of

experiencing the world;

that listening

leads to

understanding;

and

that love

is unconditional

and without

judgment.

Through Otis' eyes I see

that being playful

is feeling alive;

that things

are just things;

and

that rest

and quiet times

renew the spirit.

Through Otis' eyes I see

that it is hard

to be patient;

that life

is full

of temptations;

and

that following

the pack usually

isn't in

my best interest.

Through Otis' eyes I see

that I must let others know

how I feel in order to get

what I need;

that looking backward

prevents me from

seeing forward;

and

that poor

choices provide

good lessons.

Through Otis' eyes I see

that we are

all born with

natural talents;

that I must overcome

my fears to get

where I need to go;

and

that only by feeling

comfortable with myself

can I be comfortable

with others.

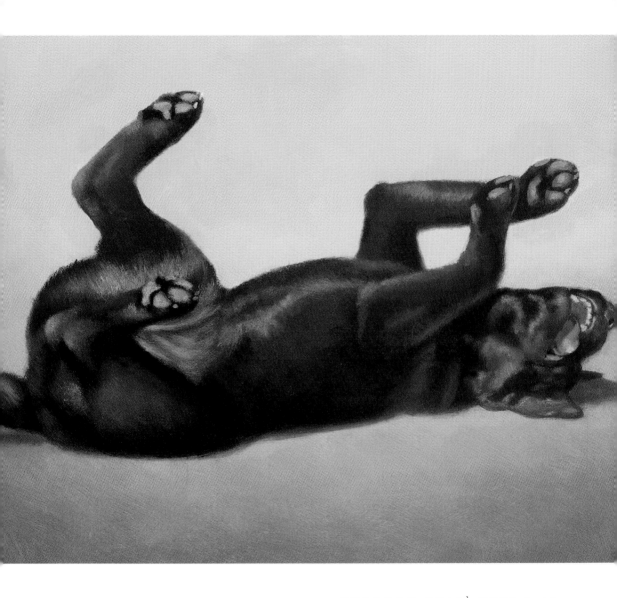

Through Otis' eyes I see

that sometimes what I see

in someone else is

a reflection of myself;

that focusing on the good

fortune of others prevents

me from appreciating

my own blessings;

and

that the more things

I have, the more

I have to worry about.

Through Otis' eyes I see

that I must look past

appearances and search

for kindness within;

that being faithful

means seeing

beyond myself;

and

that the most

valuable gift

I can give

is my time.

Through Otis' eyes I see

that I cannot let

yesterday's mistakes

and disappointments

dampen my enthusiasm

for each new day;

that life is to be

lived in the present;

and

that I should

be alert to

unexpected pleasures

and opportunities.

Through Otis' eyes I see

that occasionally I need

to be reminded that

I am not in control;

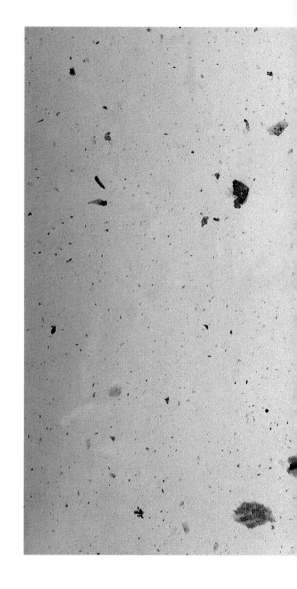

that short term pleasures

may have long term

consequences;

and

that strong bonds

are built with

love and

forgiveness.

Through Otis' eyes I see

that an awareness of

nature brings an

understanding of self;

that each one of us

is part of a

larger plan;

and

that sometimes

the needs of others

are greater

than my own.

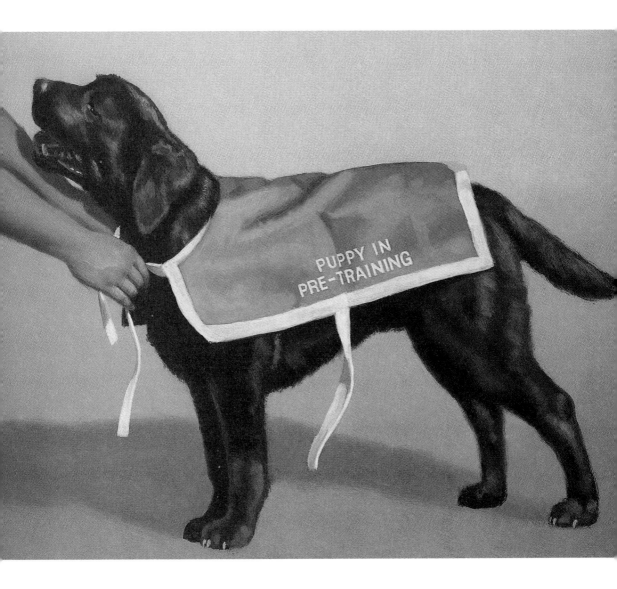

Through Otis' eyes I see

that I must trust

my own instincts

as I travel life's path;

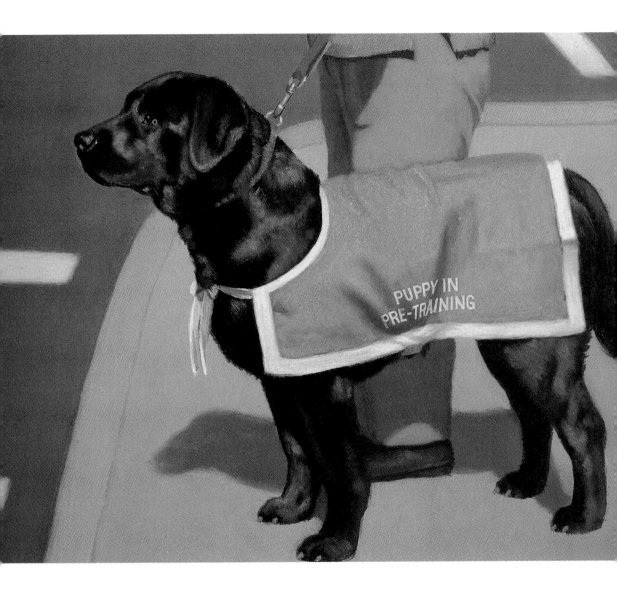

that the reward

is in the pursuit;

and

that bringing joy

into the lives of others

brings it back

into my own.

Through Otis' eyes I see

that life's hardest lesson is

learning to let go;

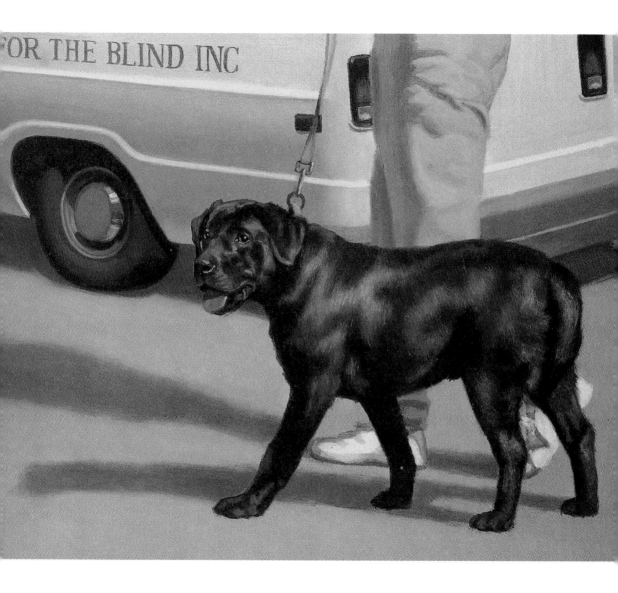

that difficult

times help

us to grow;

and

that those who

touch our lives

remain

with us forever.

Through Otis' eyes I see

that with guidance

and hard work we can

become what we

are meant to be;

that sometimes

I need a break from

what's required of me;

and

that endings

lead to

new beginnings.

Through Otis' eyes I see

that finding a purpose

beyond myself

makes life truly rich;

that the lessons of

my past guide me

to my future;

and

that helping others

gives life

meaning.

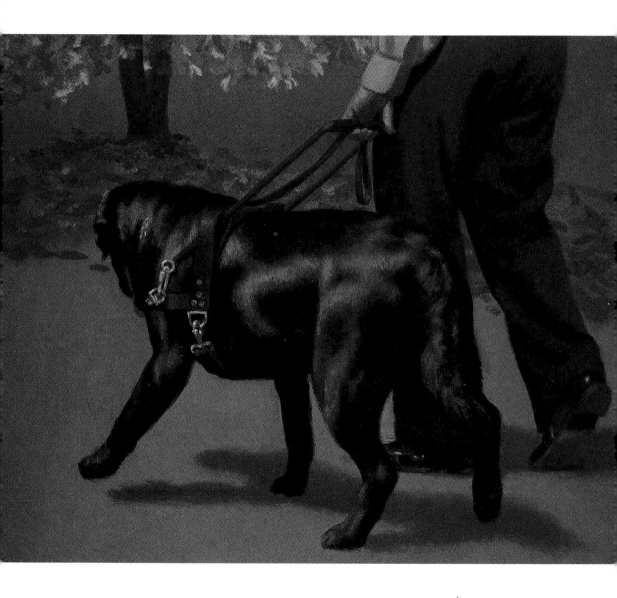

I will carry with me

always, the love I saw

through Otis' eyes.

Guide Dog Schools and Associations

Guide Dog Schools

Following is a list of guide dog schools in the United States. While not comprehensive, the list is intended to serve as a resource for blind individuals seeking a guide dog or persons who wish to become puppy raisers or volunteers.

CALIFORNIA

Eye Dog Foundation for the Blind
211 S. Montclair St., Suite A
Bakersfield, CA 93309-3165
(805) 831-1333
Area served: U.S. and International
Puppies raised in: Arizona

Guide Dogs for the Blind, Inc.
P.O. Box 151200
San Rafael, CA 94915
(800) 295-4050
Area served: U.S. and Canada
Puppies raised in: Arizona, California, Colorado, Idaho,
Nevada, Oregon, Utah and Washington

Guide Dogs of the Desert
Box 1692
Palm Springs, CA 92263
(619) 329-6257
Area served: U.S. and Canada
Puppies raised in: Alaska, Arizona, California, Nevada, Oregon,
Utah and Washington

Guide Dogs of America, Inc.
13445 Glenoaks Blvd.
Sylmar, CA 91342
(818) 362-5834
Area served: U.S. and Canada
Puppies raised in: California

CONNECTICUT

Fidelco Guide Dog Foundation
Box 142
Bloomfield, CT 06002
(860) 243-5200
Area served: New England and New York
Puppies raised in: Connecticut and Massachusetts

Southeastern Guide Dogs, Inc.
4210 77th St. East
Palmetto, FL 34221
(941) 729-5665
Area served: U.S., Canada and South America
Puppies raised in: Alabama, Florida, Georgia, Louisiana,
North Carolina, South Carolina, Tennessee, Texas and Virginia

HAWAII

Eye of the Pacific Guide Dogs & Mobility Services, Inc.
747 Amana St., #407
Honolulu, HI 96814
(808) 941-1088
Area served: Hawaii, Guam and Alaska
Trained dogs are provided by the Royal Guide Dogs Association of
Australia and the Royal New Zealand Foundation for the Blind.

KANSAS

Kansas Specialty Dog Service
P.O. Box 216
124 W. 7th St.
Washington, KS 66968
(913) 325-2256
Area served: Primarily Middle U.S.
Puppies raised in: Colorado, Illinois, Iowa, Kansas, Missouri,
Nebraska, Oklahoma and Texas

Leader Dogs for the Blind
1039 S. Rochester Rd.
Rochester, MI 48307
(810) 651-9011 or toll free (888) 777-5332
Area served: Unlimited
Puppies raised: Throughout the United States and Canada

The Seeing Eye, Inc.
P.O. Box 375
Morristown, NJ 07963-0375
(973) 539-4425
Area served: U.S. and Canada
Puppies raised in: Delaware, Pennsylvania and New Jersey

Guide Dog Foundation for the Blind, Inc.
371 E. Jericho Turnpike
Smithtown, NY 11787
(516) 265-2121 or (800) 548-4337
Area served: United States and International
Puppies raised in: Connecticut, Florida, Iowa, Nebraska, New York,
South Carolina, Vermont and Washington, D.C.

Guiding Eyes for the Blind, Inc.
611 Granite Springs Rd.
Yorktown Heights, NY 10598
(914) 245-4024 or (800) 942-0149
Area served: Unlimited
Puppies raised in: Connecticut, Delaware, Maine, Maryland,
Massachusetts, New Hampshire, New York, North Carolina,
Rhode Island, Vermont and Virginia

Freedom Guide Dogs, Inc.
1210 Hardscrabble Rd.
Cassville, NY 13318
(315) 822-5132
Area served: New York
Puppies raised in: New York and Pennsylvania

Upstate Guide Dog Association
Box 165
Hamlin, NY 14464
(716) 964-8815
Area served: Western New York
Puppies raised in: Western New York

Pilot Dogs, Inc.
625 W. Town St.
Columbus, OH 43215-4496
(614) 221-6367
Area served: U.S., Canada, Mexico and other countries
Puppies raised in: Indiana, Kentucky, Michigan, Ohio,
Pennsylvania and West Virginia

For additional information about each school, readers may wish to consult *A Guide to Guide Dog Schools*, 2nd Edition, 1994, by Toni and Ed Eames. This is available through the National Library Service in braille or cassette, or for sale in print or on computer disk from Disabled on the Go, 3376 N. Wishon, Fresno, CA 93704-4832; phone (209) 224-0544.

Guide Dog Associations

Guide Dog Users, Inc.
(Affiliate of the American Council of the Blind)
14311 Astrodome Dr.
Silver Spring, MD 20906
(301) 598-2131

National Association of Guide Dog Users
(A Division of the National Federation of the Blind)
1800 Johnson St.
Baltimore, MD 21230
(410) 659-9314

Organizations that may be contacted for information about guide dogs, hearing dogs or service dogs include the following:

Assistance Dogs International
c/o Canine Partners for Life
230 Whitehorse Rd.
Cochranville, PA 19330
(610) 869-4902

International Association of Assistance Dog Partners
P.O. Box 1326
Sterling Heights, MI 48311
(810) 826-3938

National Service Dog Center
The Delta Society
289 Perimeter Rd. East
Renton, WA 98055-1329
(206) 226-7757
(800) 869-6898 (Voice)
(800) 809-2714 (TDD)

About the Author

Patricia Burlin Kennedy was born into a family that included a retired German Shepherd guide dog. Her love and admiration for these devoted animals led her to raise Otis and to write *Through Otis' Eyes.*

Mrs. Kennedy has served for many years on the staff of the United States Senate in Washington, D.C., and as a volunteer for a variety of charities and organizations. She is also pursuing her interest in the human/animal bond. A graduate of Michigan State University, Patty lives with her husband, two children and two dogs in Northern Virginia.

About Otis

Otis is a real guide dog puppy, bred by Guiding Eyes for the Blind, Inc. He was raised by the author's family in Virginia.

About the Illustrator

Since 1961, Robert Christie has been living in Atlanta, Georgia, and painting people and their horses and dogs. It seems an unlikely life for a boy born and raised in Brooklyn, New York, but an interest in animals and years of art study seemed to guide him right into it.

Mr. Christie first studied art at Ohio Wesleyan University, after which he attended and graduated from Pratt Art Institute in his hometown. While working as a designer, he did postgraduate study at Pratt and the Art Students League in New York. During this time, in 1959, Robert and his wife Beth were married. They now have five children, three grandchildren and two sons-in-law, all in the Atlanta area.